ONE LUCKY NIGHT

a comedy in two acts

by M.J. Gallagher

ONE LUCKY NIGHT (Original Title: "Getting Lucky")
ISBN 978-1-312-38674-7
© 2004 M.J. GALLAGHER
All rights reserved.
Professionals and amateurs should know that any performance of ONE LUCKY NIGHT is subject to royalty.

Published By Mighty Gargoyle Media

For information on performance royalties and other scripts, please e-mail mighty_gargoyle@yahoo.com

Visit www.mightygargoyle.com

One Lucky Night

The Characters

Lonnie, a bar patron

Una, a singer

Colm, a friend

Kelly, a bar owner

Hugh, a beat cop

Paul, a barback

All the action takes place at **Kelly's Irish Rose**, a bar.

About the Author

M.J. Gallagher is a cartoonist, playwright, and prose author.
As cartoonist, he is the creator of The Mystery Girls comic strip. His plays *include Cindy Claus Saves Christmas, Fast Times at Holiday High, One Lucky Night*, to name a few.

His fairy and folk tales were first collected in New Magic (2002).
A former professional actor, for three years he toured as the Host of the Recycle Rex show. He has taught acting styles that include monologues, auditioning, acting for commercials and on camera situation comedy acting.

Other Books Available by the Author

Let's Make a Scene! Short Plays and Scenes for Grade School Performers

Cindy Claus Saves Christmas (Script)

Fast Times at Holiday High (Script)

Getting Lucky (Script)

The Wish-Bird, an Island Fantasy

The Jade Green Heart

Olivia & the Willow

One Lucky Night

by M.J. Gallagher

Act I

SETTING: KELLY'S IRISH ROSE, EARLY EVENING.

A simple Irish pub downtown.

Stage Right: Front door; juke box; dart board. The bar itself sits just left of center, with stools in front. There is a door behind the bar stage left, on the far wall, to the back room of the joint.

Kelly is discovered washing glasses and tidying behind the bar. A very drunk man sits on the far right stool. He is completely disheveled, and looks like he would pass out if he didn't mutter to himself.

Frank Sinatra's Saturday Night is the Loneliest Night *plays on the juke box.*

Kelly: Yeah, well you got that one right, Frank. Saturday night's sure the loneliest night around here.

Lonnie: *(Attempts to sing along with the song)*

Kelly: That wasn't an invitation for a serenade.

Lonnie: *(Muttering)* I've always liked this song.

Kelly: You're one for deep, long conversations, aren't you?

Lonnie: I don't care what anyone says, Frankie was a real nice guy.

Kelly: Oh, now don't you start. I've got better things to do than waste time talking to you.

Lonnie: ...always there for a guy a little down on his luck...

Kelly: I've got to change the tap on the keg. *(She exits to the back room.)*

Lonnie: ...he almost could've been Irish...

Enter Colm in something of a fluster.

Colm: Kelly? *(Crosses to the bar)* Kelly, ya here? *(Turns to Lonnie)* Where's Kelly?

Lonnie: *(Looking up from his whiskey and taking a good look at Lonnie.)* Ya know, you kinda look like him.

Colm: What's that?

Lonnie: Frankie.

Colm: Is she in back, then? Oh, never mind. I'll just help m'self to a pint till she gets back. *(He crosses behind the bar to the beer taps.)*

Kelly: *(Offstage)* Don't even think it, Colm McGinty! *(Enters from back room.)*

Colm: Well, what d'ye expect me to do then? Die of thirst out here? *(He crosses to the front of the bar and sits on a stool.)*

Kelly: You can wait till I've finished changing the keg, like everyone else.

Colm: What everyone else?

Kelly: Now don't you start.

Colm: Things have slowed down a bit of late, haven't they?

Kelly: Yes, but it's no concern of yours.

Colm: So, it looks like I am going to have to die of thirst after all.

Kelly: You could stand to take a night off, now and then. *(She pours a draft for Colm.)*

Colm: If I do that, you're likely to close down for sure.

Kelly: I'd still have some clientele, even without your grace's presence.

Colm: You mean him?

Kelly: He's been loyal.

Colm: I've never seen him in here before.

Kelly: Where're your eyes? He's been coming here every night for the past couple of months.

Colm: And that's the clientele you'd like to cater to...

Kelly: Sssh. He'll hear you.

They look at Lonnie, who shifts on his stool slightly, then starts muttering a Sinatra song. Kelly motions to Colm, and they move to the opposite end of the bar.

Kelly: He's kind of a strange bird, that one.

Colm: How so?

Kelly: Well, he comes in here every night at exactly the same time. Seven o'clock.

Colm: And that's strange.

Kelly: No, exactly seven o'clock. I noticed it a while back. The minute hand hits the seven and bang, he comes through the door.

Colm: Well, punctuality is a virtuous quality.

Kelly: And what would you know about virtuous qualities?

Colm: Now, Kelly...

Kelly: He's not just punctual, McGinty. He's punctual to the very second. It's not normal.

Colm: What does he do?

Kelly: I don't know. He's always a bit tipply when he comes in here. He's quiet, though.

Lonnie hums a Sinatra song.

Kelly: He seems to like the old songs.

Colm: Well, there are stranger folks who've graced the threshold of this bar.

Kelly: And you're not the least of them. *(She picks up a rag and busies herself, wiping down the bar.)*

Colm: You know, you ought to sell this bar, and settle down.

Kelly: I have settled down.

Colm: Oh, you're married now, is it?

Kelly: I'm married to the Irish Rose. Carrying on the Kelly legacy.

Colm: Still trying to please your old man, you mean.

Kelly: Are you finished with your beer, McGinty? I'll thank you to pay for it, then, and get out.

Colm: Now, Kelly, girl, don't get yourself in such a fluster at the words that come out of me mouth. Though the flush in your cheeks does bring out your eyes.

Kelly: You'll be more than flushed if you don't go on with yourself.

Phone rings.

Kelly: *(Exasperated)* Hello. Oh, hello, Gene. No, nothing's—what? But I paid that bill meself. I put it in the driver's own hands. No, don't you bother. I'll be coming down there meself. Good-bye.

Colm: What's the matter?

Kelly: Oh, the wonder of it all. The check I paid for the beer bill has disappeared, and they want me to pay it again. They'll see Saint Patrick himself first if they expect me to pay the bill twice! *(Gets sweater and prepares to leave.)*

Colm: You're leaving?

Kelly: I'm going down to the distributor and sort this out. The Rose will only be closed for an hour.

Colm: You're closing the bar?

Kelly: What, do you see a full complement of tenders and waitresses, McGinty? Of course I'm closing the bar.

Colm: I'll watch it for you.

Kelly: You? I'd sooner let that one. *(Indicates Lonnie.)*

Colm: Oh, come on. You don't want to close the bar so early on a Saturday night, do ya? Think of the customers who might actually come in.

Kelly: Now—

Colm: And you don't want to toss this poor fellow out onto the street, do ya?

Kelly: Well....

Colm: And I won't even ask you to pay me for my troubles. Consider it a favor.

Kelly: After the tab you've run up at this bar, don't think I'd be paying you at all.

Colm: It's settled, then.

Kelly: Well....

Colm: Run along now. You don't want to get there and find that they've closed for the night themselves.

Kelly: I keep a close eye on the inventory, McGinty, so don't think to drink me out of my mortgage.

Colm: *(Crossing behind the bar.)* I'll just have a couple of pints to see me through.

Kelly: One. And no more.

Colm: One, then. And a whiskey.

Kelly: One. Draft or whiskey.

Colm: Done, then.

Kelly: I'll be back in—

Colm: About an hour. See you then, Kelly.

Kelly looks back once more, then exits through the front door.

Colm: *(Pours himself a draft. Looks at Lonnie.)* She always was a softy for the hard luck cases, you know. I knew that she wouldn't turn you out. Me, on the other hand, that's another matter altogether. If I didn't pay for a pint now and then, she'd probably close down the Irish Rose just to spite me. Now, me and Kelly go back a ways. Her da and I used to play the ponies together. Ah, old man Kelly. He had quite a way with horses, ya know. His father had been a horse trainer in Donegal, and I think he must have passed something on to his son. We'd go down to the track, and he always seemed to know just who'd win. But he never put more than two dollars down. Said it wasn't right to make money out of nothing. I used to make a pretty pocket of change when I'd go to the track with Old Kelly. But, you know, it'd be gone just as quick as it came. Same with Kelly, I guess. When he died he had nothing to leave behind but the Rose. And that with a mortgage still and bill up to here... *(Notices Lonnie staring drunkenly at him.)* Here now, what are you looking at? Oh, enough of these old sad songs. Let's liven up the place, shall we? Maybe then some customers will come back. *(Colm crosses around the bar to the juke box.)* Let's see what we've got here... Sinatra... Roy Orbison... Dean Martin... Louis Prima...There isn't an Irishman in the bunch! Ah, here we go. *(Chooses an upbeat tune, then checks pockets for change.)* Damn, not a penny. I'm sure Kelly won't mind if I borrow a quarter or two to help her own business... *(He turns and Lonnie holds out his hand with a quarter in it.)* Well, that's mighty kind of you. *(He takes quarter, puts in juke box, and chooses his song.)* Say, what are you drinking there, lad? Can I buy you one? *(He crosses back behind bar.)* Whiskey is it? No doubt Kelly is savin' the good stuff. So, Bushmill's it is... *(He grabs a bottle and pours a shot into Lonnie's glass. As soon as he's finished, he realizes his mistake.)* Say now, what's this? I didn't mean to pull out the Jameson. Oh, well, she'll never—no, knowing Kelly, she'll know all right, and mark it on my tab. Well, lad, I guess that's one you owe me, then. *(The song suddenly shifts to a sad song.)* Here now! Looks like that machine is going on the blink. Kelly won't be happy about the expense of fixin' it, that's certain. *(Lonnie sings along with the song.)* You're a queer one, ain't ya? You're not one for talking much. Do you always sing like that?

Lonnie: Only when it's a sad song.

Colm: Oh, it's like that, is it? You like the sad songs. *(Lonnie goes back to singing.)* Say, what's your name, lad? Mine's McGinty. Colm McGinty. *(They shake hands.)* I figure we should get to know each other a bit if we're to be stuck here alone until Kelly gets back.

Lonnie: Lonnie. And we're not alone.

Colm: What's that?

The door opens, and Hugh enters. He is Kelly's older brother, a beat cop.

Colm: Well, what do you know? Hugh Kelly, ladies and gentlemen!

Hugh: What are you doing behind that bar, Colm? Where's Moira?

Colm: Kelly? Why, she had to step out for a bit....

Hugh: And leave you behind the bar to look after things, did she? What do you take me for? Moira!

Colm: It's the God's Honest Truth, Hugh. Kelly had to run—

Hugh: Don't call my sister Kelly. Her name is Moira.

Colm: She likes to be called Kelly. It is her family name.

Hugh: It's not ladylike. Kelly was my father. And he's gone. Moira!

Colm: I'm telling you, Hugh, she had to go down to the beer distributor. She'll be back any time, now. Can I get you a drink?

Hugh: You can get from behind that bar, you roach. That's what you can be getting.

Colm: Fine, fine, have it your way. It is the Kelly family bar.

Hugh: Now you know perfectly well that Kelly left it to Moira herself. Though why he did that, I'll never know. A girl running a bar in a city like this...

Lonnie: *(Muttering)* Lots of women run pubs. Maggie, and Irene....There was Molly O'Neill...oh, she was a pretty one...

Hugh: How's that?

Lonnie: She had such petite feet...

Hugh: What?

Colm: Oh, don't mind him. I think he's heard a few too many of those songs.

Lonnie: She'd dance...right up there on the table....

Hugh: I guess Moira really isn't here.

Colm: That's what I've been trying to tell you. How about a whiskey? It's a cold night.

Hugh: I wouldn't drink with you if you were paying for it. And we know there's about as much a chance as that happening as—

Colm: Fine, fine, Hugh. Have it your way. How is the beat?

Hugh: Chilly. But quiet. My arches will be the death of me.

Lonnie: It's your shoes.

Hugh: What's that?

Lonnie: Your shoes aren't made for you.

Hugh: What's he talking about?

Colm: Something about your shoes.

Hugh: They're police issue. The finest that the department can buy, thank you very much.

Lonnie: It's your shoes. I can fix 'em for ya.

Hugh: What's that, again?

Colm: He says he can fix your shoes. Maybe he can, Hugh. Why don't you let him try?

Hugh: Oh, you're both crackers.

Colm: Are you here for the night, then? 'Cause if you are, perhaps you'd like a nice game of dice.

Hugh: And play with a cheater like you? You keep your dice, and I'll keep my money, thank you very much.

Colm: All right. How about you, lad? You up for a game of dice?

Lonnie: Sure.

Colm retrieves a pair of dice cups from behind the bar; slides one to Lonnie.

Hugh: When did you say she'd be back?

Colm: She said she'd only be gone for about an hour. She'll be back almost any time now.

Hugh: This place is like a morgue.

Colm: It is a bit quiet, isn't it? Where d'you suppose all the customers are at these days?

Hugh: I don't know. That new bar across the street, I imagine. The Shillelagh. Fancy bar with fancy owners.

Colm: They sure seem to have grabbed the attention of the neighbourhood. *(Looks out front window)* It does look busy over there. I wonder what the draw is.

Hugh: They play Keno over there. Or maybe it's the five hundred types of beer they have on tap.

Colm: I heard it was only about eighty.

Hugh: Or the fancy cherry wood décor.

Colm: Hey, Kelly should put Keno in over here. That'd quench a thirst of a different kind.

Hugh: I don't think she would. Muther didn't think well of gambling nor gamblers. That's why Kelly never put in a lottery here. I don't think Moira would either. She's too like her da in so many ways.

Colm: But he played the ponies.

Hugh: Only because he loved horses so much. He never gambled more'n two dollars at a time.

Colm: Perhaps she could add a view types of beer. Those new microbrews are all the rage, as they say.

Hugh: A man finds one beer he likes and sticks with it. That's the normal and natural way.

Colm: Sometimes a man likes a little variety.

Hugh: You and your variety. Always flittin' about from this to that—beer to beer, flower to flower, girl to girl. That's what got you into trouble with Moira, you know. You and your variety.

Colm: Let's not have that again....

Hugh: Well, it's true. If you weren't such a flibbertigibbet, chasin' after dreams you never would work for, she might've actually settled down with you and never decided to follow in Old Kelly's footsteps. A girl her age runnin' a bar....

Colm: Well, thanks for the vote of confidence, Hugh.

Hugh: I've never had much confidence in you, Colm McGinty. Not since you swindled Old Kelly out of his winnings the last time you two went to the track together.

Colm: Now, wait just a minute—

Hugh: Well, I don't have time to jaw on what's past with you while Moira's off gallivantin' and playing at barkeep. I've got a beat to walk. Ohhh, my arches...

Hugh exits the front door. Colm stares after him.

Colm: Why, of all the—

Lonnie: He's a tight-wound one. *(Colm turns to him.)* It's his shoes. They're hurting his feet.

Colm: And just what do you know about a policeman's shoes, you singing bottle of whiskey?

Lonnie: Quite a bit, actually. I used to be a cobbler.

Colm: Well, that's no excuse for him talking to me that way. Why I ought to—

Lonnie: You have to watch the bar. Till she comes back.

Colm: I hope things are going well down at the distributor.

Lonnie: How 'bout another whiskey?

Colm: No, thanks. I'm a beer man, meself. *(Lonnie points to his own glass.)* Oh, right. *(He crosses back behind the bar and grabs a bottle; pours a shot in Lonnie's glass. Lonnie downs it as Colm replaces the bottle.)* What was your name again, lad?

Lonnie: Lonnie.

Colm: Funny, when you said it the last time, I could have sworn you said "Lucky."

Lonnie: Now don't get me started on that one.

Colm: What one?

Lonnie: Lucky the bloody leprechaun. Leprechaun indeed.

One Lucky Night

Colm: You mean the cute little fella on the box of cereal? With all the marshmallows?

Lonnie: I told you not to get me started.

Colm: Why he's a cute little gnome, ain't he? And who couldn't like the cereal. All those marshmallow charms. Yellow moons, blue stars...and green clover!

Lonnie: I said—

Colm: They're magically delicious!

Lonnie: That's it! That's why I threw my television out the hotel window! I couldn't take his smarmy little ways... and the children, always on the hunt for him, enticed by greed into kidnapping and thievery.

Colm: Why it's just a cartoon, man!

Lonnie: It's a marketing crime against a great people.

Colm: You mean the Irish? Oh, I don't think there's any harm—

Lonnie: I mean the *leprechauns.*

Colm: Leprechauns?

Lonnie: Yes, the leprechauns. As proud a people as ever there was, mocked and satirized by people who wouldn't know a true leprechaun if he came and set fire to his shoes.

Colm: Leprechauns, he says! Oh, now I've heard everything. Lucky—

Lonnie: It's Lonnie. And I'll thank you to call me that.

Colm: Lonnie, do you know what day and what age this is, man?

Lonnie: I'm well aware of the date.

Colm: Then you must know that no one—not even old Irish drunkards—believe in the wee folk any more.

Lonnie: Well, that's not the problem of the leprechaun, I'm sure. And they're not "wee folk."

Colm: They're not.

Lonnie: No. Some are small in stature, to be sure, but there's quite a range in sizes and girths, let me tell you. Some are at least as tall as you, or I.

Colm: Oh, you've seen them, have ya? I suppose they all come over for Sunday dinner with you and your mother.

Lonnie: Not anymore. Not for a long time.

Colm: I can see it now. Little men, with little green jackets and little green bowlers, jumping up and down on your furniture! I hope they brought a nice bottle of wine, at least!

Lonnie: I'd watch what I'd say if I were you. You don't know what you're talking about. The leprechauns are not the silly little elves that you are that cursèd cereal company paint them out to be. They are a proud and dignified member of the Sidh Clans.

Colm: The Sidh?

Lonnie: The Folk. What you would call Faeries.

Colm: Now it's the faeries, is it? I didn't know that leprechauns had little gossamer wings.

Lonnie: They don't. You don't know much about your fellow countrymen, do you?

Colm: My fellow countrymen, he says!

Lonnie: The Sidh have lived side-by-side with the Irish since the Celts landed on Eire.

Colm: So, you've seen them, I take it.

Lonnie: Of course I've seen them.

Colm: Friends with 'em, you might say?

Lonnie: Yes of course. In my time, many.

Colm: So, then, you know where they hide their pot of gold, then? No offense, but from the looks of you it doesn't seem that you've seen much gold.

Lonnie: Gold! That's all you ever care about is gold! The leprechauns don't care about gold! They're not as greedy as you make them out to be. We just take lightly to it when someone tries to swindle us out of what's rightfully ours.

Colm: We?

Lonnie: Never mind.

Colm: D'ya think you're a little leprechaun, is that it? Oh, you really have had too much to drink, lad. I think it's time for me to cut you off. *(He reaches for Lonnie's shot glass, which is full of whiskey again.)*

Lonnie: Just let me finish this one. *(He sips a little.)*

Colm: All right. I've never been one to let something fine go to waste.

One Lucky Night

Lonnie: Accept your talents, perhaps.

Colm: My talents.

Lonnie: You've a way with the gab and a way with getting people to do things for you. It's no little talent, that. You should be using it to make the world a better place for the people that you love.

Colm: Oh, now I'm getting advice from a little leprechaun.

Lonnie: Your problem is that you love her, but you're too stubborn to admit it. Either to her, or to yourself.

Colm: Who?

Lonnie: Kelly.

Colm: What? You're crackers for sure.

Lonnie: Oh, really. Then you come in here every night for the company of the clientele.

Colm: How do you know I come in here most nights?

Lonnie: I've been coming here nigh these two months now.

Colm: That's right. That's what Kelly said. How is it that I've never seen you in here before, then?

Lonnie: I have a common face. Perhaps I got lost in the crowd. *(Downs whiskey.)*

Colm: What crowd? This place hasn't had a crowd in it since a month after Old Kelly's wake.

Lonnie: How long ago was that?

Colm: Six months ago.

Lonnie: And the place has fallen on hard luck ever since, then?

Colm: No, it did fine at first. Busier than ever, actually.

Lonnie: So what happened to the customers?

Colm: They just stopped coming in after a while. I suppose they went to that new pub across the street, The Shillelagh. I can't understand it, though. Everyone loved Kelly behind the bar.

Lonnie: She's a natural innkeeper. I've known many like her. She was born to keep a tavern.

Colm: Well, I guess that's what Old Kelly thought. He left the place to her.

Lonnie: So the new bar took all the patronage, ya say. How long ago was that.

Colm: Well, it opened before Old Kelly passed on. But they stopped coming in only about two months ago, now, I'd say.

Lonnie: Oh.

Colm: Things aren't going well for the old girl, that's for sure.

Lonnie: She doesn't look old to me.

Colm: I mean the Irish Rose, of course! Old Kelly worked here sweeping up as a lad, and ended up buying the place forty years ago. Before he got married, even. He met his wife here. Ah, there was a couple.

Lonnie: Agnes, was it? Kelly looks just like her mother.

Colm: How did you know that? Mrs. Kelly died over a year ago.

Lonnie: I... I saw a picture of her.

Colm: Funny that. Kelly doesn't talk about her mother much.

Lonnie: I guess it's been so slow. She got tired of talking to the walls.

Colm: You know, when I first saw you, I thought you were an old sot, but you seemed to have livened up a bit. Kelly talk to you much, then?

Lonnie: Some.

Colm: Anything... about me? May bar tab, I mean.

Lonnie: A little, I suppose.

Colm: Would you like another? *(Grabs Jameson bottle and goes to pour another shot. Lonnie's glass is already full.)* That's strange... I could have sworn... Let's... let's have some music, then. This quiet gets to me.

Colm comes from around bar and crosses to the jukebox. He reaches into his pocket, and again realizes that he has no change. He turns around, and Lonnie's hand is already extended, proffering a quarter.

Lonnie: Play *My Wild Irish Rose*, if you would.

Colm: *(Takes quarter, puts it in jukebox.)* I don't see it here. Oh, well, how about a little Bobby Darrin, then?

Colm crosses away from the jukebox a bit, and My Wild Irish Rose *rises from it. He stops, turns to Lonnie, and looks at him. Lonnie quietly sings along.*

Lonnie: *(Singing along.)*

Colm: You—you—you—

Lonnie: What?

Colm: You *are* a leprechaun!

Lonnie: Now, wait, you said yourself—

Colm: The whiskey—I knew I didn't fill it but once m'self.... and the jukebox...

Lonnie: I... I don't want any trouble....

Colm: But you can't be... Where's your little green hat and four leaf clover?

Lonnie: Oh, you're asking for it, you are. I told you, we don't wear cute little green outfits. We look just like you, if we've a mind to. As a matter of fact, my clan colours are scarlet and brown, thank you very much.

Colm: A bleeding leprechaun!

Lonnie: Now... now hold on, lad... I don't like that look in your eyes... I don't have any gold, if that's what you're after. I told you, we aren't a greedy lot, like yourselves....

Colm: Do something else.

Lonnie: What?

Colm: Do something else, just so I can be sure that I'm not going over the deep end.

Lonnie: Oh, bother with you....

Colm: Disappear into thin air. That's what they always do on the television when they want to prove that they are real.

Lonnie: Right now I'd rather you disappear into thin air and let me finish my whiskey. *(Downs whiskey.)*

Colm: Do something, leprechaun, or you'll get no more whiskey from me.

Lonnie: If I waited for you to fill me up when I was thirsty, I'd be dead and shriveled into a raisin now. *(He holds his hand over the shot glass, and it fills with whiskey.)*

Colm: By all the saints....

Lonnie: I'm guessin' it's a long time since you've been inside a church, with all the faith you've got, Colm McGinty.

Colm: He knows my name, even!

Lonnie: You introduced yourself to me not half an hour gone.

Colm walks around Lonnie warily.

Colm: Thank goodness for that, at least.

Lonnie: What are you on about, now?

Colm: It's said that if you catch a leprechaun and hold him, he owes you a wish....

Lonnie: Oh, not that, now. You don't know very much about the us....

Colm: I know enough—

Colm rushes at Lonnie and grabs him in a half-nelson. They struggle a bit. Lonnie is unable to get out of the hold.

Lonnie: No. You don't know anything. That's plain. Leprechauns don't go about granting wishes to every johnny that mugs them. We don't grant wishes at all, for that matter.

Colm: Then what good are you?

Lonnie: That's glory for you, isn't it? In my time, I've helped out plenty a family by giving them what they need to carry them through the day.

Colm: What's that? Food? Gold? Jewels?

Lonnie: No, you greedy-hearted bastard. Shoes.

Colm loosens the hold a bit.

Colm: Shoes?!?

Lonnie: Yes. And I'll thank you to take your hands off me.

Colm: Not till I get that wish.

Lonnie: Wish-schmish.

Lonnie elbows Colm in the torso. Colm lets go and holds his own stomach.

Colm: Ow! You tricky little snake!

Lonnie: That should teach you to lay hands on someone who's just trying to mind his own business. Now, sit down and I'll tell you a thing or two about Clan Sidh. *(Colm sits. He takes a drink from his beer on the bar.)* The Leprechauns are a simple but proud folk, and we haven't taken kindly to all the propaganda that's been perpetrated against us.

Colm: But—

Lonnie: Ah. Ah! We're not the little mischief-makers that your Hollywood has made us out to be. We're cobblers.

Colm: Cobblers.

Lonnie: That's right. We make shoes. We always have. Why, we made riding boots for the Tuatha de Dannan themselves, when they ruled the land. Not a Daoine Sidh goes to a royal cotillion but that he wears a dancing shoe made by our hands.

Colm: Is that where does the gold come in, then?

Lonnie: It'll come out of the teeth in your head if you don't hush up.

Colm: Some of the stories have to be true, don't they?

Lonnie: There might be an original grain of truth in them, but it's grown into such a jungle of misconceptions it breaks my heart to think of it. You humans are so afraid of what you don't understand that you'll make up stories about a person, rather than simply ask him to explain his ways to you.

Colm: I'm asking now, Lonnie.

Lonnie: Smart lad. Now, it's true that we've been well-paid for our efforts, but over the centuries business dwindled to the point where we had to go to you humans for our customers. But even that didn't last.

Colm: So you make shoes?

Lonnie: Not me. Not any more.

Colm: Why not?

Lonnie: You heard the story *The Shoemaker and the Elves* when you were but a babe, I'm sure?

Colm: You mean that was you?

Lonnie: Not personally, mind you, but it's a tale that has happened, after a fashion. Only my clan was so hungry for any kind of shoe-making work that they actually signed up as employees in this—I can't believe it—Englishman's shoe company! English, do ya hear? And being Irish, of course, he paid them well below the going wage. I refused to follow my brothers into that servitude. So I stuck out on my own.

Colm: Stuck out on your own?

Lonnie: It was a sorry time for Ireland and the Irish. The blight had spread from farm to farm to farm, and people were starving to death—literally in the streets, lad. Men were fleeing the island, mostly to England at Liverpool. But many came here to the States. Most of my clan went to England, where a shoe manufacturer by the name of Collier was offering positions with his company. Some positions. Factory work for barely a living wage. We were masters of our craft, d'ye understand? Artisans of the highest order, one and all! I couldn't join my brothers in such servitude. So I traveled around Ireland on my own for a few years, taking what work I could get. But there wasn't much, let me tell you, so finally, like millions of other Irishmen, I boarded a vessel and came to America.   That voyage across the sea was one of the most horrific journeys that anyone has ever taken. The squalor and the filth. The desperation. Whole families trying to hold on to life while the stores of food on board dwindled. Holding on with the hope that in America, the land of liberty and opportunity, they would find their livelihoods again.

Colm: It is a great country.

Lonnie: Aye, that it is, but not for everyone, all the time. Oh, sure, the Irish have their parades now, but when we first came here, we were treated little better than slaves. It's like that with each wave of immigrants. I've seen it time and again.

Colm: When... when did you come here?

Lonnie: 1880 or '81. It's tough to recall, exactly.

Colm: Faith and feathers! How old are you, then?

Lonnie: Let's see... on me last birthday I turned just two hundred and thirty-two years old.

Colm: By all the saints!

Lonnie: I take it I'm older than I look?

Colm: You're older than anyone looks!

Lonnie: Well, I've got several older brothers...

Colm: I need a drink.

Lonnie: Me, too. Shall I go on? Or have you had enough—

Colm: No, no, go on. Please.

Lonnie: At first the Irish could only get the most menial jobs. Cleaning sewers, keeping stables, picking fruit and the like. But at least they could feed their children, after a fashion.

Colm: Did you find any work in your profession here in America?

Lonnie: I thought about it at first, but I decided to travel and see some of this great continent.

One Lucky Night

Colm: So, where have you been?

Lonnie: I think I went to Long Island once.

Colm: What? No further?

Lonnie: Well, you see now, I didn't just come to New York because everyone else on the bleeding island was coming here.

Colm: The why did you come

Lonnie: I came because this is where my girlfriend was.

Colm: Your girlfriend? A young leprechaun in love, were ya? I'm sorry, man. Who was she? Another leprechaun?

Lonnie: No, she came from another clan of the Sidh.

Colm: Which one?

Lonnie: Bean Sidh.

Colm: Banshee? Aren't they hideous old ghosts who howl or some such?

Lonnie: No. The Banshee are members of the folk. Each banshee is attached to a human clan. Her job, as it were, is to herald the death of a member of that family by singing her song. So as to get them prepared of the Coach of Death that will take them away to the other side.

Colm: You make them sound so friendly.

Lonnie: *(Shuddering slightly)* Oh, they're anything but that.

Colm: So, why—?

Lonnie: One day, about a century and a half ago, I was walking along the shores of Donegal, right by an ancient baronial castle. The sun was setting over the ocean. Ah, it was a glorious sight. So I decided to stop and watch the sunset while I worked on the heel of a shoe I was making for the local priest. Suddenly, I felt the wind change direction. I looked up the cliff just north of the castle to see this... this vision of a girl floating near the edge of the cliff. The sun had caught her red hair and set fire to it. Her eyes—like stars right before the dawn, they were. And she had these rosy cheeks, and the most darling cupid bow smile. The breeze had pulled her gown, dark grey like a storm cloud it was, taught against her curves.

Colm: Wow.

Lonnie: The she opened the petals of that little rosebud of a mouth, and let out the loudest, most brain-piercing eagle cry from hell. It was the most frightening thing I'd ever heard in my life. It made my teeth hurt and, if I remember correctly, I fell off the rock I was sitting on and hit my head on another. I've still got a scar.

Lonnie shows Colm a scar under his hairline.

Colm: And you went out with her anyway?

Lonnie: I was in love, already. If only she had screamed her death wail before I had a chance to lay eyes on her...

Colm: So, off-hours like, she's a lovely girl, then?

Lonnie: She's a hellcat. The worst temper of any woman, faerie, or beast that has ever walked the earth. And she doesn't just scream. Make her mad, and she throws things.

Colm: Throws things?

Lonnie: She hit me square on the side of the head with an iron once. Thrown at ten feet. *(He shows Colm another scar.)*

Colm: Jesus and Mary—so it didn't last long, then?

Lonnie: Oh, we were together, on and off, for going on a hundred and twenty years.

Colm: A hundred and twenty years??

Lonnie: Give or take.

Colm: But why—

Lonnie: *(Eye to eye with Colm)* If you saw her, you wouldn't have to ask the question.

Colm: So why did you two break it off then?

Lonnie: Most Banshee live near the ancestral homes of the families for which they are harbingers. But Una—

Colm: Una?

Lonnie: *(Wistfully)* Una... When the last member of the family that lived in Ireland died, she didn't want to be cooped up in a drafty old castle all alone. So she packed up and came to America to be near the last surviving members.

Colm: And so she lives near them now.

Lonnie: Not anymore. The last one died off about twenty years ago, and so she found herself sort of...

Colm: Out of a job?

Lonnie: Exactly.

Colm: Another victim of 80s downsizing. *(They laugh.)* So then what happened?

Lonnie: Well now, Una was always a wandering spirit at heart. It's one of the things we had in common. She decided it was time to go "find herself." She started hanging around with artists and writers and... *(bitterly)* musicians.

Colm: Musicians?

Lonnie: A bass player at that. You know, that line "I play a little bass," has been used on more impressionable young women... Una actually decided that was going to perform for people.

Colm: Perform? You mean sing?

Lonnie: She started getting bookings in small clubs in the Village. Most nights, she'd clear out the entire house before the end of her first number.

Colm: I'm not surprised.

Lonnie: She came to the conclusion that I was the one holding her back—crowding her creativity, she called it. No doubt quoting words from that long curly-haired saxophone player...

Colm: I thought it was bass.

Lonnie: Find herself! Two thousand years old, and she's off to "find herself!"

Colm: Two thousand??

Lonnie: And that's not the worst of it!

Colm: It's not?

Lonnie: After twelve decades of being in love with a banshee, hearing her wail day in and day out—

Colm: I thought she only did that when someone was about to die.

Lonnie: Oh no, she had to practice, each and every morning in the bathroom. "Just in case," she said! Have to keep the vocals ready!

Colm: Good God.

Lonnie: Now, even though I'm free of her and her frightful ways, I hear her cry in my dreams, every night.

Colm: You have nightmares.

Lonnie: You have nightmares. These are more than that, and far worse. What I'm hearing is the harbinger of my own death. *(He grabs Colm's arm.)* First, off in the distance, comes the sound of some bird screeching in the night. **(SFX)** It comes closer, until I realize it's the wail of the banshee. But it's not as though I'm listenin' to someone else's death knell... it's my own... **(SFX)** Did you hear that? There it is... I can hear it now—**(SFX)** You can here it, can't ya, lad?

Colm: I... I don't hear anything, Lonnie.

Lonnie: It's so horrible, Colm! **(SFX)** You must've heard that! *(Lights change, SFX horse hooves off in the distance.)* And there, coming this way—the Dullahan! *(SFX whip, horse, carriage moving swiftly. Lights turn red and green.)* The Coach of Death! The driver is whipping his phoukas into a frenzy! *(Lonnie moves to center, and kneels on the floor.)* They're coming for me, Colm—they're coming for me!

Colm: *(Meeting Lonnie on the floor.)* You've got to get a hold of yourself Lonnie. There's nothing coming! There's no one here but you and me.

There is one last banshee wail, and the green and red lights flare brightly for an instant. Lonnie screams. All lights fade to dim.

Kelly enters, swinging open the door widely.

Kelly: What's this then? *(Switches on the lights.)* What are you up to, Colm McGinty. With the lights off?

Colm: Kelly, you're back!

Kelly: And what are the two of you doing on the floor? *(Lonnie curls into a ball and whimpers.)* He's in a bad way. what did you do to him, Colm?

Colm: I didn't do anything to him. We were only talking—

Kelly: Fine talk, I'm sure. Look at his eyes. He looks as though he's seen a ghost.

Colm: A banshee, more like it.

Kelly: What's that he's sayin'?

Lonnie burbles in Gaelic.

Colm: Lonnie....Lonnie, can ya hear me?

Kelly: That's his name, then?

Colm: Lonnie, it's me, Colm. Can you hear me?

Lonnie: They will ride the winds of storm/Their fury will be felt/ Before time their kind was born/ They bring darkness through the light...

Kelly: Just talking, were you?

Colm: Yes, that's all it was.

Kelly: *(Kneeling to Lonnie)* Lonnie, it's me, Kelly.

Lonnie: The fire that burns cold will rise up from the depths. They will ride the icy white horses!

Kelly: Oh, the poor, mad fool.

Lonnie: *(To Kelly)* Una? Have ye come back to me? Una?

Kelly: Who's Una?

Colm: His girlfriend.

Kelly: Girlfriend?

Colm: Ex.

Kelly: Lonnie, I'm here. Kelly. It's Kelly. Moira Kelly.

Lonnie: Kelly? Oh, I... oh, Kelly.

Colm: I think he's snapped out of it. Nothing like a woman's touch. *(Kelly shoots him a sharp glance.)*

Lonnie: What am I doing on this floor?

Colm: *(Helping Lonnie to his feet.)* You got a little excited, tis all. Lonnie, Kelly's back. *(Lonnie turns to her.)* Kelly, this is Lonnie.

Lonnie: Happy to make your acquaintance at long last, Miss Kelly.

Kelly: Thank you...Lonnie. Are you going to be all right, then? Perhaps we should take you to a doctor.

Lonnie: Oh, that won't be necessary, I assure you. I'll be fine.

Kelly: I don't know...

Lonnie: I think I'd like to sit down for a while, if you don't mind.

Colm: By all means.

(Lonnie crosses to barstool; sits.)

Kelly: Well, you're "shift" is over, Colm. I think you've done enough for one night.

Colm: You're welcome for watching the place while you were gone.

Kelly: I didn't thank you.

Colm: So. How did it go?

Kelly: Oh, fine. Not only did the driver lose the check, but they said there was an unpaid balance from last year that they just "re-discovered." They want me to pay $1500.00 more by Tuesday.

Colm: Good Lord.

Kelly: That'll seriously cut into the mortgage payment this month. With the way things have been going here, I haven't had any money to spare. I don't know where I'm going to get it.

Colm: Something will turn up, Kelly. You won't lose this place.

Kelly: Oh, really? That makes me feel so much better. Your words of empty comfort won't pay my bills, Colm.

Colm: I was only—

Kelly: You were doing what you always do, Colm. Make nice talk. "Things will be okay. Every cloud has a silver lining." You live your life as if, just by wishing it, things will turn out. You're a grasshopper, Colm, playing your fiddle in the summer and not thinking about what you'll do when the winder comes. You live from moment to moment, and you don't put anything away for the future. And now, because of it, I'm going to lose this bar.

Colm: What have I got to do with that?

Kelly: I—I meant Da. You two were peas in a pod, you were. I only wish he'd put some savings away, in case something like this happened. Oh, Colm, I'm sorry. I shouldn't have taken this out on you.

Colm: That's all right, Kelly. I understand. Right now you can take anything you want out on me. You need to.

Kelly: No, right now I've got to figure out where I'm going to get the money for the mortgage *and* the distributor bills. Oh, I can't blame Old Kelly, either. It's not his fault that people stopped coming in here.

Colm: *(Looking out front window.)* It must be that new bar across the street.

Kelly: No, I don't think so, Colm.

Colm: Why not?

Kelly: The clientele at the Shillelagh is a bit different from ours.

Colm: How so?

Kelly:	You haven't been over there, have you?
Colm:	No, of course not. The is Irish Rose is where I call home.

Enter HUGH.

Kelly:	Hello, Hugh.
Hugh:	Moira, I cannot believe that you left your livelihood in the hands of someone like Colm McGinty.
Kelly:	He couldn't do anything worse to it than I've already done.
Hugh:	What do you mean?
Kelly:	Nothing. How's the beat?
Hugh:	Quiet, except for some hoodlums that broke into Zabrowski's corner market.
Colm:	Did they get anything?
Hugh:	Friends of yours, Colm?
Colm:	You're just full of laughs lately, aren't ya, Hugh? *(He crosses to Lonnie.)*
Hugh:	What's wrong with that one?
Kelly:	He had some sort of spell, I guess you'd call it. He'll be fine.
Hugh:	Want me to call the wagon for him?
Colm:	That won't be necessary, Officer Kelly. I'll take care of him.
Hugh:	He'd be in better hands down at the precinct, I think.
Colm:	Oh, and since when did you start thinking, then?
Kelly:	That's enough, boys. He'll be fine, Hugh. Do you want some coffee to take with you on patrol?
Hugh:	That'd be lovely, Moira.

Kelly pours coffee into a paper cup, hands it to Hugh. He puts several heaping teaspoons of sugar in it.

Kelly:	Lonnie, would you like some coffee?
Lonnie:	Never touch the stuff.
Hugh:	Why am I not surprised? Well, I'll be on my way, then. I just wanted to make sure you got back all right.
Kelly:	Thanks, Hugh.
Hugh:	How did everything go?
Kelly:	It went—fine. Everything went fine. Good night, Hugh.

Hugh: Good night, Moira. *(Begins to exit.)*

Colm: Good night, Hugh! *(Hugh stops, gives Colm a look and exits.)* Sometimes I can't believe we were friends once.

Kelly: He still resents you.

Colm: Oh, he thinks I ran your father into the ground, you mean.

Kelly: No, McGinty. He resents that you and Old Kelly grew to be more like father and son than they did.

Colm: What?

Kelly: It's true. Hugh was always closer to Mother. He and Da never did things the way the two of you did.

Colm: Well, sure'n it's not my fault—

Kelly: I'm not saying that it is. But I think he feels... well, like he never got a chance to tell Kelly how he felt.

Lonnie: It's a tough thing for a son to tell his da all the things he truly feels.

Kelly: Old Kelly thought the world of Hugh, even if he thought he was too rigid of mind. But he loved him dearly, as any father would his son. But, you know he thought of you as his son, too.

Colm: The feeling was more than mutual. My own da died when I was just a tyke, ya know. I never knew him.

Kelly: All this talk of death is making me miss the old dog all over again. And it's making hard to stay angry at him!

Colm: Like you ever could. Look, I'm hungry. What's say I go out and get us a few sandwiches from around the corner?

Kelly: Why, Colm McGinty, I think you've struck gold with that idea.

Colm: D'ya want to come along with me, Lonnie?

Lonnie: I think I'll stay here for right now, if it's all the same to you.

Colm: Fine, fine. I'll be back before you can say "Lucky the bleeding leprechaun."

Colm exits. Lonnie turns to look after him just as Colm has cleared the threshold.

Kelly: So, you and McGinty seem to have struck up a friendship.

Lonnie: He's a good man.

Kelly: Well, I don't know if I'd go that far—

One Lucky Night

Lonnie: You know, I knew a girl just like you when I was young.

Kelly: When you were "young"?

Lonnie: Well, younger... She had the same colour to her eyes...except her hair was darker. Men from miles and miles around came to her inn just to see her. She was that beautiful.

Kelly: You think I'm beautiful, do ya?

Lonnie: Of course, and I'm not the only one. But you also share the same quality—you both speak your mind. And you be loved for it.

Kelly: Well, I—where was this, did you say?

Lonnie: A town called Letterkenny, in Donegal.

Kelly: Why, that's where our whole family is from.

Lonnie: What kind of sandwiches d'ye suppose he'll get?

Kelly: Oh, he knows just what I like on a sandwich.

Lonnie: Is that right?

Kelly: Sure.

Lonnie: You've known him a long time, then.

Kelly: Oh, since I was about fifteen. He used to come around and sell the Racing Forum to Kelly's customers when he was a lad.

Lonnie: He was like a paper boy, then?

Kelly: He also used to collect the old men's bets and take them to a bookie.

Lonnie: Is that what he is now? A bookie?

Kelly: No, he stopped doing that after awhile. He's never held a job for very long. He has no perseverance.

Lonnie: Wasn't the money good? Running numbers for a bookie?

Kelly: Oh, sure. But he got tired of it, I suppose. Or too interested in my mother's cooking.

Lonnie: Your mother's cooking?

Kelly: Old Kelly brought him home one Sunday night for supper. They got on famously. Soon after that Colm was over most Sundays at our house. He and Da would stay up for hours, talking and arguing. Finally, Mother would send me out to tell Colm to go home, and Kelly to go to bed.

Lonnie: And Colm would leave?

Kelly: Well, sometimes, if the night was nice, I'd walk him home. It wasn't too far. And, other nights, if it were cold, like, we'd wit in front of the fire, and argue ourselves...

Lonnie: You don't do that anymore?

Kelly: Well, we're older now. I've been busy running the bar. And... and he's been busy, too.

Lonnie: Doing what?

Kelly: Gambling, I suppose.

Lonnie: Well, a girl like you should certainly set your sites higher than a rake like that.

Kelly: Now wait a minute, I never said—

Lonnie: So, it wasn't like that, then?

Kelly: Well... for a while it seemed like it was going to be. He ... he asked me to marry him, once.

Lonnie: But you said "no."

Kelly: I didn't give him an answer. I told him I'd have to think about it. Then Kelly... died, and I couldn't think about anything but running this bar.

Lonnie: How did he die, Moira?

Kelly: Mother... Mother had been ill for a long time, and died about a year ago. After that, Kelly wasn't himself. You could tell he was withering away, but holding on to something. He got so old in the last few months. I hated to see him like that. But Colm was over every night, and he took him to the track just like they used to. He seemed to enjoy that. He loved horses. Then, one morning we found him in bed. So still. He was holding his rosary, and mother's photograph.

Lonnie: I'm sorry.

Kelly: I'm not. Not really. He's where he truly wants to be, with his Agnes.

Lonnie: Sweet Agnes.

Kelly: Why, that's what he used to call her. Exactly. Sweet Agnes. When I was a kid, sometimes I used to come sneaks downstairs on Sundays. Mother and Dad would be here in the bar, all alone, dancing to some tune on the jukebox. Sometimes it would be Vic Damon, or Louis Prima, and Dad would whirl her around so, and she'd laugh, and then he'd

	laugh, and they'd whirl around together, getting dizzy, like schoolchildren they were! Then sometimes, they'd be dancing slowly, pressed tight against one another...just slowly swaying to some quiet song by some crooner.
Lonnie:	Like Frank Sinatra.
Kelly:	Yes. She loved Frank Sinatra. Said he was the only man she'd ever leave Kelly for. Then she'd pause and look at Da. She'd go over to him and take his face in her hands and say "Now how could I ever leave such a homely one as this?" When they were dancing, all slow and swaying, Da would be touching Mother's hair, all blond and catching the light like I've never seen anyone else's do. And he'd call her Sweet Agnes...Oh, look at me go on so!
Lonnie:	You've got her hair. And her smile.
Kelly:	How did—?

Colm enters, carrying a bag of sandwiches.

Colm:	If I didn't know better, I'd say you two were wooing.
Kelly:	Colm McGinty, of all the things—!
Colm:	*(Crossing to the bar.)* Pastrami with extra hot mustard and a pickle for the lady. And a club sandwich for the lep—for Lonnie.
Lonnie:	You're a gentleman to be sure.
Kelly:	How much, Colm?
Colm:	I am shocked and offended. Did I ask for payment?
Kelly:	Why, thank you. You're a chipper one tonight.
Colm:	It's a chipper night!
Kelly:	Is it, now? What have you got brewing in that scheming brain of yours? *(She takes a pint and crosses to the tap.)*
Colm:	I have been thinking of my lady's plight and I have come up with a plan.
Kelly:	A plan. Oh, I'm not at all sure I'm going to want to here this. What is it?
Colm:	It's a secret.
Kelly:	A secret. *(She tries to pour a pint.)* A secret plan that you can't tell the owner of the bar you'd like to save.
Colm:	Let's just say I'd have to check out all the angles first.

Kelly: Curse this thing! I just changed the keg! I'll go check on it. *(She exits to the back room.)*

Colm: So what were you two talking about, then?

Lonnie: About this and that.

Colm: This and that. Well, it looks like you two were pretty cozy.

Lonnie: Well, she's a beauty. And if you won't have her, then...

Colm: So there is something going on between the two of you.

Lonnie: Well, it's not like you have any claim on her yourself, eh, lad?

Colm: No, of course not.

Lonnie: Good, then. I think she's taken quite a shine to me, doncha think? You'd be surprised what a woman would do when someone brings a little magic into her life.

Colm: And what kind of magic would that be, hmm? All the shoes she could ever want?

Lonnie: That works for more than you can imagine.

Colm: I can't see Kelly going out with a down-on-his luck leprechaun, can you?

Lonnie: *(Laughing ruefully.)* "Down-on-his -luck." Aye, that's true enough....there's a reason for the phrase, the "luck of the Irish." They're not just words.

Colm: I don't follow.

Lonnie: A friend of the Sidh has a good luck charm for life.

Colm: Pardon?

Lonnie: One of the characteristics of the Sidh is that we exude a kind of fortune, good or ill, that can be bestowed on people, or a place. Unless....

Colm: Unless?

Lonnie: There's really only one way for a leprechaun to lose his ability to bring fortune to others.

Colm: And how's that?

Lonnie: When he loses his love, he becomes, as you said, down on his luck

Colm: Hey, wait... Kelly said that you'd been comin' in here every night for the last two months. That's just about when

	things started to go downhill for the Irish Rose. *(Pause.)* Say, Lonnie....
Lonnie:	Well...
Colm:	Well, what?
Lonnie:	I fear that I may be the cause of the poor lass' woes of late.
Colm:	You mean that just by hanging out here at the Irish Rose...
Lonnie:	...I've brought such ill-luck to this pub that it may be ruined.
Colm:	Then why've you been hanging out here?? Do you have something against Kelly?
Lonnie:	Oh, no, not at all, lad. The Irish Rose is the closest thing I've got to calling a home, is all.
Colm:	Well, your home isn't going to be around for long if we don't do something. Isn't there some way to reverse you luck again?
Lonnie:	I don't have any control over it. I suppose... if I were to fall in love again. But that seems unlikely.
Colm:	But you've had your eyes on Kelly.
Lonnie:	Kelly? Well, she's fair to be sure, but she's not the woman to replace what Una took from me.
Colm:	You know, Lonnie. Maybe we can help each other out.
Lonnie:	Help each other out?
Colm:	Yeah. On my way to the deli, I started thinking. You're in a rut. I'm in a rut. Kelly's certainly in a rut. More like a bind. We need something to get us out of our ruts.
Lonnie:	And what might that be?
Colm:	A little bit of magic.
Lonnie:	Oh, now—
Colm:	Listen! You know how people these days go crazy for anything resembling the supernatural. And you're the real thing!
Lonnie:	Colm, I don't like where this is heading.
Colm:	What you need, Lonnie, is to take control of your life again. Strut your stuff.
Lonnie:	What is it that yo want me to do? Make shoes for people again?

34

Colm: Maybe later. But you can do other things. I saw you. The drinks. The jukebox.

Lonnie: Aye, some small talents here and there.

Colm: Exactly! People will love what you can do. And on top of it, you've got all those stories.

Lonnie: What, you want to put me on display?

Colm: Only for a night. Now don't look like that. It'll be easy.

Lonnie: Easy, he says.

Colm: Look, we'll throw a party. Canvas the neighbourhood with invitations. You'll do some tricks, tell some tales of the Emerald Isle.

Lonnie: I don't know, Colm. I'm not much of a performer.

Colm: What are you talking about? You're a natural. A supernatural! Look, Kelly's about to lose this place. She needs some cash. Fast. Now, to my reasoning, you're sort of responsible for the shape the bar's in.

Lonnie: Not all by myself.

Colm: You owe it to Kelly. We both do.

Lonnie: Well...

Colm: It'll be fun! I know I can get some girls to show up.

Lonnie: Girls, ya say.

Colm: Sure, it'll be just the thing to get you back into the swing of things.

Lonnie: It does sound grand, in a way. I haven't been to party in quite a long time.

Colm: You'll be the guest of honour. And Kelly will be so grateful.

Lonnie: I'll do it, Colm.

Colm: That's the spirit, Lonnie! Now, come on, we've got some errands to run.

He grabs Lonnie by the arm and pulls him off the bar stool.

Lonnie: Hey, wait, let me grab my sandwich.

Lonnie grabs the sandwich from the bar. He takes the last swig of his drink.

Lonnie: We've got flyers to design, and we have to stop by a costume shop around the corner....

Lonnie: Costume shop?

They exit.

Kelly enters from the back room.

Kelly: Well, you wouldn't believe what had happened to that keg. I don't know how the hose came off. I had to find a clamp—say now, where did you boys run off to?

Blackout.

ACT II

Scene 1: Later that night.

Lights up. Hugh is discovered in shirtsleeves and apron behind the bar. "I Will Survive" plays over the jukebox. Hugh washes glasses to the beat of the song.

On the coat rack stage right hangs Hugh's police jacket and hat.

The phone behind the bar rings.

Hugh: Kelly's Irish Rose. Oh, it's you, Colm. No, Kell—*Moira* ain't here. I don't think that's any concern of yours. Oh, she said she had to go to the bank. No, I don't know what for. To make a deposit, I suppose. How should I know when she'll be back? Do ya have a message? I have to get back to work. Be here around seven. Right. Yes, I'll tell her if I happen to think about it. Good night.

He hangs up the phone.

I wonder what kind of trouble he'll get Moira into now.

The door opens and a young man enters.

Top o' the evening, lad. What'll it be?

Paul: Wow, you've really got the authenticity thing down, haven't you?

Hugh: I beg your pardon?

Paul: The accent, I mean. It's really good.

Hugh: Accent?

Paul: Yeah. I take acting classes at NYU. I took a dialect class last semester. My name's Paul. I'm a barback at the Shillelagh, across the street.

Hugh: Oh, that bar.

Paul: Have you been in? We've only been open a couple of months. *(He spies Hugh's police jacket and hat on the coat rack.)* Wait, now I recognize you. You're that cop that walks a beat around here, aren't you? I didn't know you

One Lucky Night 37

	moonlighted as a bartender! Isn't that some sort of conflict of interest?
Hugh:	This is my sister's bar. I'm just helping out while she runs an errand.
Paul:	Oh, good. I'd hate to see you get into any sort of trouble.
Hugh:	And what can I be doing for you then?
Paul:	Oh! I came over to see if I could get some change. We've had a really busy night, and it's the weekend, and.... anyway, do you have fives for this fifty?
Hugh:	I don't know.
Paul:	Well, could you check? I'd really appreciate it. I mean, we.
Hugh:	One moment... *(He crosses to the cash register and opens it. He takes the fifty from Paul and gives him fives.)* Here you go, then.
Paul:	Thanks a lot. You've made my whole life a little easier.
Hugh:	Uh-hunh.
Paul:	So... what time will you... get off?
Hugh:	Just as soon as the owner gets back. *(Pause)* Why?
Hugh:	Well, you've been so helpful... I was just wondering if you'd like to come over to the Shillelagh later for a drink. My treat.
Hugh:	I don't think the Shillelagh is my kind of pub.
Paul:	No? That's funny, I would have thought... Well, if you change your mind, I'll be there all night. I hope you'll change your mind. Well, good night, Officer...
Hugh:	Kelly. Like the bar.
Paul:	Kelly. Of course. How blond of me. Well, good night, Officer Kelly.
Hugh:	Good night, then.
Paul:	Paul. Not "then".

He exits.

Hugh:	Fancy bar, with fancy barbacks. As if he thinks I'd ever be seen in a place like the Shillelagh. "Paul, not then." What's that supposed to mean, then? "How blond of me." Silly flibbertigibbet.

Colm enters with Lonnie.

Lonnie has been dressed in a vest and bow-tie, both green. He sports a green bowler and a Shamrock pin. Colm has a large banner rolled under his arm.

Hugh: Now why is he dressed up like a clown?

Colm: Clown? Haven't ya ever seen a leprechaun before, Hugh?

Lonnie: I can't believe you talked me into this.

Colm: You said yourself I've got a way about me.

Lonnie: Yes. And you should bathe more.

Colm: Hugh, I'd like to introduce you to the Irish Rose' very own leprechaun: Lonnie.

Hugh: I knew you were crackers, Colm, but I didn't know how much.

Colm: We're havin' a big party tonight to introduce everyone to the leprechaun. It'll be a smash!

Hugh: How so? No one is going to believe that this spindly little drunk is a leprechaun.

Lonnie: I take offense to that.

Hugh: Being called a drunk?

Lonnie: No, spindly.

Hugh: Well, sorry then, your leprechaunlyness.

Colm: Oh, Hugh, you've never had faith in anything in your life. By the time we're done tonight, not only will the people of this neighbourhood believe in leprechauns, but they'll believe that their wishes can come true, and the Irish Rose will be saved.

Hugh: You'd have more luck if you passed out gold coins.

Lonnie sits down on his stool. Colm crosses to Hugh at the bar.

Colm: Here, take the other end of this.

Together they unfurl a large banner that reads: GET THE LUCK O' THE IRISH. BUY A PINT, HAVE YOUR WISH COME TRUE.

Hugh: Oh, Saints preserve us....

Colm: Help me hang it on the front of the bar. I've already hung one outside the door.

Hugh: You mean people will see this from the street???

Colm: Of course! It's called advertising.

Hugh: It's called silliness, if you ask me.

Colm: I didn't hear anyone askin' ya.

Hugh: Does Kelly know about this?

Colm: Do ya think I'd go to all this trouble if she didn't?

Hugh: I think you'd do plenty to ruin her life.

Lonnie: I'm thirsty.

Hugh: Oh, that's news.

Colm: Just give our the man a drink, Hugh, will ya? After all, he's the guest of honour.

Hugh: *(Pouring whiskey)* More like the roach of honour.

Colm: That's unkind of you, Hugh.

Hugh: I'm sorry if I hurt the little faerie's feelings.

Lonnie: You didn't hurt me nothin'. If you did, you'd be sorry for certain.

Hugh: Are you threatening an officer of the law?

Colm: Behind that bar, Hugh, you are a bartender. The both of you should just cool your coals. For Kelly's sake.

Lonnie: & Hugh: For Kelly's sake.

Colm: Now then, I have to go see if my flyers are done and hand them out if they are. Can the two of you play nice until Kelly returns?

Lonnie: I can if he can.

Hugh: I suppose.

Colm: Fine! Don't get too drunk, Lonnie.

Lonnie: With himself pouring, it's a sure bet that I won't.

Colm exits. There is an uncomfortable pause.

Hugh: So. What's this scheme that the two of you have concocted?

Lonnie: It's all Colm's idea. He wants me to do some tricks.

Hugh: Put on a show, like?

Lonnie: Something like that. Could I have another?

Hugh: What? Already?

Lonnie: It was a small whiskey.

Hugh: *(Smugly)* Colm said he didn't want you to get drunk.

Lonnie: *Too* drunk, he said. He doesn't want me to get too sober, either. Or I might change my mind about doing this whole shindig.

Hugh: So perhaps you should pace yourself better.

Lonnie: Oh, hang it.

Lonnie magically pours himself a whiskey.

Hugh: What by St. Agnes' goodness was that?

Lonnie: Well, if you aren't going to serve me, I'll just have to serve meself.

Hugh: How'd you do that?

Lonnie: It's just a trick.

Hugh: Where did it come from?

Lonnie: From your own whiskey bottle. *(Hugh cross to check the well whiskey.)* No, the good stuff.

Hugh: *(Checking the Jameson bottle.)* You're right. It *has* gone down! *(He looks queerly at Lonnie.)* So, you're a magician, then...

Lonnie: Something like that.

Hugh: Do something else!

Lonnie: No, not right now. I have to save it up for tonight. After all, I'm out of practice.

Hugh: Aw, c'mon. If you're rusty, you might as well practice right now.

Lonnie: I don't know...

Hugh: *(Crossing to front of bar)* Come on, now. I love magic!

Lonnie: All the Irish love magic.

Hugh: When I was a little kid, I used to have a magic set. I put on shows for my Mother and Dad, and my aunts and uncles. After dinner, I'd put on my cape, one that Mother had made for me, and open my magic box. It was one of Mother's old hatboxes that she gave me. I called myself "Hugh-dini!" Then I'd do card tricks for them all. Card tricks were always the most popular. And I'd show 'em all how to stand an egg on its end. I was so into being a magician. Mother encouraged me. She thought I'd be a great showman when I grew up. She used to put me to bed with stories all about Irish faeries and elves and witches, good and bad.... She even told me that she had a personal friend who was a leprechaun. Imagine, a mother telling that to a child! But, I believed all that she told me, and that I thought it was real for a while. So real, that I thought I could learn to do real magic. One time, when I was about seven, I tried an experiment. I locked the door to the bathroom upstairs in our apartment, and I tried to unlock it using magic! Mother had told me that all witches can unlock locked doors, and I wanted to be able to do it. To become a witch. I gestured and I concentrated. I came up with my own incantations. *"Oh, wooden door that is shut tight, open under my magic might!"* Oh, Dad had to climb up and crawl through the small outside window into the bathroom to unlock the door. He searched for me for hours, but I hid under his bed and he never found me. I think he threw out my magic kit after that....Can you make a dove appear out of a handkerchief?

Lonnie: Now why would I be wanting to do that?

Hugh: Well then, what can you do?

Lonnie: I really shouldn't.

Hugh: Please. Perhaps you could even teach me some tricks. I haven't done it since I was a kid. Will you need an assistant at the party?

Lonnie: It's not that kind of magic. If it got out of hand, you'd only have yourself to blame.

Hugh: Oh, you probably can't do anything else. You're just a sham, as I thought.

Lonnie: Do you like to dance?

Hugh: *(Sitting on barstool)* Dance? Me? No...

Lonnie: Why not?

Hugh: Well, I've got bad feet, for one thing.

Lonnie: You don't have bad feet. You have bad shoes.

Hugh: Is that right?

Lonnie: Yes. *(He crosses in front of Hugh and kneels down.)* Now, first.

Hugh: Hey, what are you doing there?

Lonnie: *(Fiddling with Hugh's shoes)* Poorly constructed—absolutely atrocious. Whatever happened to pride in workmanship?

Hugh: Hey!

Lonnie: There now. How do they feel? *(Lonnie pulls away to reveal that Hugh's shoes have been magically transformed to another pair.)*

Hugh: St. Peter's beard...How'd you do that?

Lonnie: Try 'em out.

Hugh: *(Standing, he walks a bit.)* Say... it's like I'm walking on a cloud!

Music from the jukebox rises. It plays "To Be Real."

Lonnie: Why don't you try 'em for dancin'.

Hugh: I don't... *(takes a couple of dance steps)* Hey... these really do feel good. *(Music rises more)* I feel like... I could do this forever!

Hugh begins to dance in earnest as Lonnie pours himself another drink.

Enter Paul, the barback from across the street.

Paul: Wow, you're a really good dancer.

Paul dances over toward Hugh.

Hugh: Now, see, I don't really dance....

Hugh suddenly leaps atop the bar and dances like a go-go girl.

Paul: Well if that's not dancing, then someone call the fire department, 'cause girl, you are on fire! I hope you come by tonight after your shift. We're having this great dance contest. With those moves, you're sure to win!

Hugh: What is it that you came over here for?

Paul: I came to see if there was anything you needed from our bar. Change. Whatever. Just returning the favour.

Hugh: We don't need anything from your fancy little bar. Now, if you'll excuse me, I have work to do. *(Hugh grabs the bar rag from his back pocket, bends over and starts to wipe down the bar, all the while dancing.)* Thank you and good night.

Paul: Well, okay... hope to see you later....

Hugh: *(Forcibly)* Good *night*.

Paul exits.

Lonnie: You're sure to win that dance contest at the Shillelagh tonight.

One Lucky Night

Hugh: *(Jumps off the bar and tries to force himself to stop dancing)* What have you done to me???

Lonnie: Why, I've done nothing, lad. Only fixed your shoes.

Hugh: It's these shoes, all right. *(Hugh tries to take the shoes off)* They—they've done something to me. I can't stop dancing! And where did that music come from? You...you're--!

Hugh manages to pull off one shoe. He falls onto a bar stool.

Lonnie: Just a shoemaker, lad.

Hugh: Shoemaker... Shoemaker, my Aunt Fanny! You're a leprechaun!

Lonnie: So you noticed how I'm dressed, then.

Hugh: Not that kind of a—My mother used to tell me bedtime stories about the little people—

Lonnie: Enough of your offensive terms.

Hugh: The leprechauns were ones who went around making shoes... and getting into mischief...

Hugh pulls off the other shoe. The spell is completely broken.

Lonnie: The only mischief I've gotten into lately is what your friend Colm is drummed up.

Hugh: Colm McGinty is no friend of mine.

Lonnie: But he was once, wasn't he?

Hugh: Once, perhaps.... But that was a long time ago.

Lonnie: What happened?

Hugh begins to walk around in his stocking feet, carrying his shoes.

Hugh: When he first used to come around the bar, Mother didn't like him. Dad always did, even when he came in to sell things. He'd sell anything. Knock-off perfumes. Flowers. Newspapers. Gadgets. Jewelry. Mother used to have Da run him out if she thought he was selling anything illegal. But he had this... this way about him. I always thought he was lucky.

Lonnie: Lucky.

Hugh: Yeah. He was completely free. He could go where he wanted, do what he wanted, with no one to answer to. And no matter what he did, people couldn't help liking him. Even my mother. He grew on her, I guess. I always thought there was something... something special about him. Till he

Lonnie:	threw it all away on a whim and conned my father into squandering his life's savings in the bargain.
Lonnie:	And how did he do that?
Hugh:	Oh, he urged Da to take all his money and bet it on a horse. It lost, of course.
Lonnie:	Which horse?
Hugh:	I don't know. Nor do I care. Colm McGinty took the hearts of my family and broke them. Da died when he lost that money. And there's barely been enough to keep this place going ever since. I don't know why Kelly doesn't sell it.
Lonnie:	Because it's her home. Everyone needs a home, Hugh.
Hugh:	This is a bar, not a home. And it won't even be that if Kelly can't find the money to pay the mortgage. Hey, now....
Lonnie:	*(Wary)* Now, what? Tell me more about your Da—
Hugh:	Enough talk. If you really are a leprechaun— and I think you are—*(He crosses menacingly toward Lonnie.)*
Lonnie:	No, Hugh Kelly... No—

Hugh lunges for Lonnie.

Hugh:	Gold! Mother always said that if you can catch a leprechaun, he'll take you to his gold!

They move in a circle like wrestlers preparing to grapple with one another.

Lonnie:	Stay back, Hugh Kelly. 'Tis true, a leprechaun I be, but you'll find catching me no easy trick. One step closer, and it's a faerie strike you'll be gettin', not gold! *(He gestures meaningfully.)*
Hugh:	A faerie strike? *(He backs away a bit.)* Aw, you're bluffin'—

He advances. Lonnie gestures as if throwing something at Hugh, who jumps back as if struck by something on the arm.

Hugh:	Hey, wait a minute... that barely hurt!
Lonnie:	*(Desperately)* The next one won't!

Hugh advances, then stops and looks at the door.

Hugh:	Oh, McGinty. You're back.

Lonnie turns to the door. Hugh lunges savagely and puts Lonnie into a police hold, like a full nelson.

Lonnie:	Augh! You deceitful—

They struggle. In the struggle, Lonnie loses his bowler.

Hugh: Oldest trick in the book! Now I've got you! Where is your gold?

Lonnie: Oh, by Maeve's white hair. There is no gold, you lummox. Not let off!

Hugh: Not until you show my your gold.

Lonnie: Didn't you hear what I just said? I have no gold!

Hugh: Of course you'll say that, to try to trick me.

Lonnie: Oh, for Brigitte's sake. Let off, or there'll be hell to pay, to be sure. Colm won't like this!

Hugh: Oh, he won't will he? *(Lonnie tries to step on Hugh's instep.)* You're a squirmy one, aintcha? Well, I don't have to hold on to you to have captured you....

With effort, he drags Lonnie towards the back room behind the bar.

Lonnie: Where—where are ya puttin' me?

Hugh: Someplace where you can cool off until you decide to tell me where the gold is.

Lonnie: I have no gold! I told you...what? No, don't! I cannot take dark places such as that!

Hugh: You'll be cozy till you come to your senses.

Lonnie: No, Hugh, don't *Please!* Don't put me—

Hugh pushes him into the back room and shuts the door. He locks it.

Hugh: You can't get out, either. The door's made of iron, which legends say bar your passage!

Lonnie: *(Screaming offstage)* Let me out, Hugh Kelly! Please! I cannot take small dark places, I tell you! Please!

Hugh: When you tell me where you've hidden your gold.

Lonnie: All right! I'll tell ya! It's under the cash register!

Hugh: *(Looking under register)* Thought I'd fall for that, didja?

The sound of faraway horse hooves can be heard.

Lonnie: Please, Hugh Kelly! In honour to your father's memory, let! Me! Out!! *(The horse hooves rise. Carriage sounds)* They're coming—I can hear them—they're coming!

Hugh: What's that? Who's coming?

Lonnie: The Durlahan! Coming for my soul! Hugh Kelly! Let me out!

The sound of the horse hooves and carriage rise. Lonnie pounds on the door from inside the closet. He screams long and loud, ending it in a weak gurgle. Hugh listens at the door.

Hugh: Calmed down, then? Good.

Colm bursts through the front door.

Colm: I must have passed out two hundred flyers! I'm thirsty!

Hugh: You're always thirsty.

Colm: Tonight's a special night. I can feel it. Not even your sarcasm can affect me, Hugh! *(Colm crosses to the bar, notices Lonnie's hat on the floor.)* Say, what's this then?

Hugh: What's what, then?

Colm: Where's Lonnie?

Hugh: Oh, he stepped out for a bit.

Colm: Oh. He dropped his hat. *(He crosses to the bar, and notices half-empty whiskey glass.)* Hugh...where's Lonnie?

Hugh: I told you. He stepped out.

Colm: He'd never've "stepped out" and left a whiskey half drunk! Where is he??

Hugh: How should I know???

Colm: Hugh, if you've done anything to him—cop or no—I'll clock you six ways till Sunday!

Hugh: I haven't hurt him. I just... detained him.

Colm: What?? Why?!?

Hugh: Well....

Colm: So you know, doncha? You know he really is a leprechaun.

Hugh: Yes. And it's me that going to get—

Colm: Where is he?!?!?

Hugh: Well.... *(He looks towards the door of the back room.)*

Colm rushes to the back room, unlocks it, and throws open the door.

Colm: Lonnie! Lonnie, are you all right??

Hugh: Of course he's all right. I told you, I didn't hurt him.

Colm: Oh, my god....

Hugh: What is it?

Colm: Didn't hurt him, Hugh?

Colm pulls Lonnie out of the back room.

Colm: Lonnie, are you all right? Lonnie... Lonnie... answer me...

Lonnie is delirious and can barely stand. He mumbles in Gaelic, then breaks away from Colm violently. He thrashes about the room in a tremendous seizure-like fit. Colm and Hugh approach him, but Lonnie lashes out with a couple of "faerie strikes" which hit them like unseen electricity. In his fit he knocks over the table and chair and finally throws himself into the air and lands on the bar. He convulses violently, then becomes very still.

A second later, having trouble getting up, he crosses to the bar.

The lights change to purple and green hues. SFX of horse hooves and carriage comes from offstage.

Colm runs to Lonnie. He checks for a pulse.

Colm: Oh my god, Hugh. Do you know what you've done? He's dead. You've killed Lonnie. You've killed our leprechaun!

The horse sounds rise, now accompanied by the wail of a woman. Hugh looks around, and cringes against the bar.

Hugh: Holy saints preserve us....

Blackout.

SCENE 2: A BIT LATER

Lonnie lies still, on his back, atop the bar. Colm in front of the bar. Hugh crouched behind the bar, out of sight.

Kelly enters through the front door. She rips off her overcoat and throws it at the coat rack, up stage right.

Kelly: What in the world is this banner doing hanging over the door? I swear, Colm, if this is one of your— Ohhh, never mind. That I'll deal with later. Of all the blasted things to happen! I can't believe it! What, am I cursed all of a sudden? You'd think the Bank of Manhattan, which has been around oh, only about a hundred years, would have figured out by now how to keep accurate track of a person's account. There is no way under God's blue heaven that I can be overdrawn. They'd better have this fixed by Monday, when the next mortgage payment is due. Beer distributors losing checks...the bank claiming I'm overdrawn...where is all this money going? And to add insult to injury, I snagged

	my coat on a nail when I turned the corner! The tailor had better be able to mend it. My favourite overcoat! *(Beat)* Colm, why is Lonnie atop my bar? Sleeping? Where's Hugh?
Colm:	He's not sleeping, Moira....
Kelly:	Moira, is it now? Well, aren't we getting familiar again, all of a sudden. Not sleeping? Good, then have him get off that bar and wipe it down. I run a clean business, if not a profitable one.
Colm:	Kelly...Moira...Lonnie...Lonnie's—

Hugh pops up violently from behind the bar.

Hugh:	He's dead! DEAD! And I killed him!
Kelly:	He's not dead.
Colm:	He is, Moira.

Kelly crosses to the bar and inspects Lonnie's "corpse."

Kelly:	He can't be...this is just like before...he'll come out of it. Won't you, Lonnie? He's not breathing... I can't feel a pulse.
Hugh:	He's gone. Gone! And it's all my fault. That poor little leprechaun, never harmed no one, and I kill him... kill him out of my own greed...now all the curses of the little people will be upon me....
Kelly:	Hugh, what are you blathering about?
Colm:	It's the other thing, Kelly. Lonnie is...was...a leprechaun.
Kelly:	A leprechaun. Well, yes, that certainly makes sense out of everything. Are you all daft?!?
Hugh:	I'll be hunted by three-headed dogs...no place outside of a church will be safe for me. I've got to get to a church.
Colm:	Kelly, listen. Lonnie really was a leprechaun. A shoe-making elf. He was over 200 years old. He told me himself.
Kelly:	Of all the things I've thought about you, Colm McGinty, gullible has never been one of them.
Colm:	He didn't just tell me, Kelly. He showed me.
Hugh:	And me! He gave me these beautiful new shoes—whipped 'em up like magic in from of me eyes. Such a giving soul he was. He gave me these shoes—oh, how light I feel in them! And instead of thanking him for them, I attacked him to get his gold. And I killed him—oh, I killed him! *(Hugh gets on*

his knees, takes a rosary from his pocket, and starts to say the series of prayers.) Hail Mary, full of grace....

Kelly goes to him.

Kelly: Hugh, you've got to get a hold of yourself. I've never seen you like this. You're was white as a sheet.

This is all insane and you are both crackers. Are you trying to tell me that when a man tells you he's an elf, you are one to believe him now? Is this some sort of sick joke that the two of you are playing on me? It's not the least bit funny, and I'll have none of it! After the day I've had, this is more than I need. Don't you dare— This is *not* happening to me. *None* of this is happening! I *am* paid up with the distributor. I am certainly *not* overdrawn at the bank. I *will* pay the mortgage on Monday and not lose my bar. And there is not, I repeat, *not* a dead leprechaun lying in state on top of my bar!

Everyone freezes for a couple of beats.

Colm: *(Tentatively)* Kelly....

Kelly falls into Colm's arms, distraught. He holds her.

Kelly: Oh, Colm! How did this happen? There's a corpse in my bar! Not that it's going to be my bar for much longer. I was behind on the mortgage payment the last two months. If I don't get the money to the bank on time this Monday, that's it! They'll take it away from me. The bar, the building, my home. And it's all my fault. Maybe Hugh was always right. I'm not cut out to run a business like this. Dad'd never have let this happen! Is there a curse on my? (Looks at Colm. She pulls away from him.) No. There's no curse. This is all your fault, Colm McGinty. Somehow this is all part of your doings. Are you trying to ruin me, so that you can control me? Have me fall into your arms like some Harlequin romance heroine, is that it? You somehow snatched the check for the beer distributors. Got into my bank account...took money from me! What would Old Kelly say if he could see you now, you dog. What would he think of you stealing from his daughter?? He was like a father to you himself, he was! You...you're lower than a dog...you're vermin... gutterslime... Give me back my money, Colm! Give it back, or I swear I'll be taking it out of your own hide!

She lunges at him and hits him on the chest. He just stands there and takes it.

Hugh: Stop it, Moira! Stop it! This isn't Colm's fault!

Kelly: You're defending him, Hugh? You should be arresting him!

Hugh: He's done nothing wrong this time. I swear. Kelly's is cursed—curse by the ire of the little people, for I've killed one of their own!

Colm: Kelly, listen. Hugh's right. Sort of, anyway. Kelly's has been under a sort of curse, but not because Lonnie died. Remember how things here started taking a downturn about two months ago?

Kelly: Yes, but—

Colm: And when did you say that Lonnie started frequenting the Irish Rose?

Kelly: About the same time....Are you saying he cursed me? Cursed the very place I call home?

Colm: I'm not sure, but I think so, in a way. Lonnie really was a leprechaun, Kelly. He told me that for most leprechauns, good luck follows them and surrounds the people they associate with.

Kelly: This is good luck?

Colm: No, let me finish. Lonnie wasn't like other leprechauns. He lost what he loved in this life, and after that, ill luck surrounded him. I think that's why you've been having all these problems. The check getting lost. Your account. The lack of customers. I think Lonnie was responsible for it all.

Kelly: I'll kill him. *(Moment of realization as she hears what she's said.)* The poor man...leprechaun. He was a funny sort, but I felt like he was part of this place. Perhaps because he's been one of the few regulars that have been coming in here. Do you think that now that he's gone, things will go back to normal?

Still on his knees, Hugh assumes a position of attention and looks straight out as if he's entranced and possessed.

Hugh: She will ride the winds of storm/Her fury will be felt/Fire, cold and burning, will rise up from the depths/She will ride the icy white horse of death!

Lyric banshee wailing in the distance. Everyone can hear it.

Kelly: What's that?

The banshee wail increases.

Colm: Holy saints preserve us....

The lights change to purple and green hues. There is the sound of horse hooves as the wailing increases.

Kelly: Colm, what's going on?

Colm: I didn't really think she'd come....I mean, I dropped off a note at that club The Feather Touch when I saw a poster for her show. But I didn't think she'd actually show up.

Kelly: Who, Colm?

Hugh is nearly frozen in the position of a prostrate, with arms outstretched at forty-five degrees from his body. He opens his mouth as if to cry out, and from him comes forth the wail of the banshee.

Hugh: The harbinger from Hell. She's comin' to get me; to exact her revenge for killing her kin. Mother always said that the worst thing you could do was harm one of the little people. She'll destroy us all! Oh, lord, protect me! Don't let her take me down to Hell! *(He goes back into his trance.)* She will ride the winds of storm/Her fury will be felt

Colm: She's here for Lonnie. His mate. She's a banshee. Oh, I think we're in for it now.

The banshee wailing crescendos. The entire place is rocked as if by an earthquake. The lights change to red.

The front door is blown open. Silhouetted by red light from offstage in the frame of the door is a woman, hair being blown wildly about. There is a final scream that comes from both The Banshee and Hugh.

The bar is flooded in blood red light for a few moments, then lights up as normal.

Everyone is discovered pretty much in the same position as they were before.

Hugh: Holy Mary, mother of God!

Una: No, but close enough.

Colm: We didn't mean to...I mean, Hugh never meant...Oh, please have mercy on us, Banshee, for Lonnie's death.

Una: Oh, don't be so over the top. He's not dead.

Colm: Yes, he is!

Kelly: Colm, is she...?

Hugh: The stuff nightmares are made of. The harbinger of death....

Colm: Kelly, that is—or was—Lonnie's girlfriend.

Una: Hey, he catches on quick. You're the one responsible for Lonnie being in such a state, aren't you?

Una crosses to Hugh.

Colm: *(Trying to distract her from Hugh.)* Now don't blame Hugh. You're the one who was giving him night terrors. He was afraid of his own shadow. His poor heart couldn't take it. I'd say that you were more responsible for poor Lonnie's misfortune and death than anyone else, you she-demon.

Una: *(Staring menacingly at Colm.)* It's baen sidh, not *she-demon*. Now back off. *(Colm is pushed back by a mystic force.)*

Hugh: Whatever you do to me, do it quick, I beg you.

Una: I should do more than freeze you in that silly position and make you say ridiculous things.

Hugh: I didn't mean to harm him. I swear.

Una: Blah blah blah you just wanted his gold blah blah blah. Yeah, I know. I've heard it before. You people and your greed. I never got that. But then, I was used to seeing you on the way out, for the better part of my life.

Hugh: I never would have put him in that closet if I thought it would mean his death.

Una: Don't you people listen? He's not dead.

Colm: There was no pulse.

Una crosses to Lonnie.

Una: Here, let me see...*(Una examines Lonnie.)* Wow... he's pretty far gone...

Colm: See?

Kelly takes a closer look at The Banshee.

Kelly: She looks familiar....

Una: Una.

Kelly: Excuse me?

Una: *(Turning to her)* I'm Una.

Kelly: Una—?

Una: Just Una. *(She crosses and takes a quarter-page announcement for her show out of her belt.)*

Kelly: Oh, Una! I've heard of you. You were big in the eighties, weren't you?

Una: Oh, she's a charmer. Keep her.

Colm: What about Lonnie?!?

Una: What about him?

Colm: You said he was pretty far gone.

Una: Oh, yeah.

Colm: Well??

Una: Well, what?

Colm: Is he... you know....

Una: Well, he's closer to death than you or I, that's for sure.

Colm and Hugh: Oh, God.

Una: What are you getting your panties in a bunch for?

Colm: He's dying!

Una: Gee, I thought you'd be happy. It's a better state than the one you thought he was in a few minutes ago.

Colm: Is... is there anything you can do?

Una: What do I look like, a nurse?

Colm: We should take him to a hospital.

Una: Oh, yeah. And what, do you think human doctors can cure a sick Sidh? I mean, once they get a look at his green blood....

Kelly: His blood's green??

Una: No, but wouldn't it be a kick if it were?

Colm: You've got to *do* something.

Una: Me? Why?

Colm: Because of what I said before. I don't think Lonnie would be so fragile if you hadn't put some kind of...of spell on him. He was already coming apart long before tonight.

Una: Well, if I did do that to him, why should I help him now?

Colm: Well... you're his girlfriend aren't you?

Una: Was. Like, way history. He walked out on me twenty years ago.

Colm: Waitaminit. He said that you left him.

Una: What?!? Figures. No, he left me when I started making it big. Couldn't handle me being successful, and him out of work, I guess.

Kelly: Just like a man.

Una: You tell me about it. Why, he even accused me of sleeping with my sax player! As if!

Kelly: They always find some excuse, don't they?

Una: I mean, the guy was mortal. I am so not into people who die, ya know? Talk about taking your work home....Oh, and that long fusilli pasta hair... *(Shudders.)*

Colm: Well then, that must be why you're not into Lonnie—cause he's dying as we speak.

Una: Oh, by Melmoth's mile-long beard.... *(She crosses to Lonnie.)* Hmm.... can I have some whiskey?

Colm: I don't think this is a time to be drinking—

Una: Not for me, for *him.*

Colm nods to Kelly, who crosses behind the bar and picks up a bottle of the good stuff and a shot glass..

Una: No, give me the whole bottle.

Kelly: The whole bottle? Do you know how much this stuff costs?

Una: Would you rather have a dead body on your hands?

Hugh hurriedly gives the whiskey bottle to Colm, who gives it to Una. Una holds the spout under Lonnie's nose, and begins to chant in Gaelic. The lights change to blue and green hues. Her chant gets louder, until she is shrieking.

Kelly: Good God!

Lonnie bolts to a sitting-upright position. Lights return to normal.

Lonnie: Brigit's Fire, woman! do ye have to go like that every morning?

Colm: Lonnie, you're back!

Lonnie: Where am I?

Una: Here, this'll help ya remember. *(She hands the bottle to Lonnie, who drinks copious amounts.)*

Colm: You okay now, Lon?

Lonnie:	*(Cheerily)* Oh, much better, thank ye, Colm. *(He gets a look at Una.)* You!!! *(He scrambles off the bar to get away from her.)*
Una:	*(Smiling widely)* Why, Avalon Duncan O'Shea! I thought you'd forgotten.
Lonnie:	Una! What's she doing here??
Una:	I heard there was going to be a party here. Apparently, I missed the party arc....
Lonnie:	Get her away from me.
Una:	Oh, that's a fine how'd'ye do to the person that just saved your life.
Lonnie:	More like ye put it in mortal peril!
Una:	I can't help it if you're overcome by the charms of a beautiful woman.
Lonnie:	With the voice of Satan himself!

They begin to move closer to one another.

Una:	Voice of Satan? Why you shiftless unemployed little boob!
Lonnie:	Glass-shattering magwitch!
Una:	Drunken good-for-nothin' bogtrotter!
Lonnie:	Vicious screaming hellcat!
Una:	Paranoid worry wort!
Lonnie:	Harpy!

They are suddenly in each other's arms, schmecking.

Una:	Oh, Avalon, I've missed ye so!
Lonnie:	And I you, Una! I should never have left you. I'm so sorry.
Una:	No, you shouldn't have. I was so hurt. That's why I cursed you with the night terrors. But the past is the past. Oh, Lonnie, if only ye'd been there by me side.
Lonnie:	I've followed your career all the while, my night blossom. I have all your albums.
Una:	You do?
Lonnie:	Yes.
Una:	That song I used to revive you is off my latest album, "Wake the Dead."
Kelly:	*(Deadpan)* Wow. This is so romantic.

Hugh: *(Crying)* I think it's...it's absolutely beautiful! *(He begins to blubber like a schoolgirl reading a romance novel.)*

Lonnie: What are ya doin' here, Una?

Una: Some guy came by the club where I'm performing and dropped off a stack of these flyers. *(She pulls out a flyer announcing the party at Kelly's.)*

Colm: Well, it was only a few blocks away, and I happened to see a poster in the neighbourhood, announcing her show...

Lonnie: I felt so guilty all this time, Una. I never stopped loving you.

Una: Nor, I, you. I forgive you, Avalon. I love ye.

They kiss. Warm golden light shines throughout the bar.

The spell on Hugh is broken. He gets up, takes out a hankie, wipes his eyes and blows his nose resoundingly.

The phone rings. Kelly answers it.

Kelly: Hello? What? Why, why yes! Please! We'd love to have you! Yes, we'll be open!

Colm: Who was that?

Kelly: A friend of Old Kelly. He's having a reunion of his army buddies, and the place there were going to have it in just burned down!

Colm: And they're coming here?

Kelly: Yes! Forty-five of them. They'll be here in half an hour!

Colm: Twenty-five times four pints a head, at three dollars....

The cash register drawer suddenly springs open with a ding.

Kelly: That's strange.... *(Kelly crosses behind the bar. She tries to put the drawer back in, but it comes off in her hand and tips over.)* Oh, blast! Of all the luck-- Say, there's something taped underneath this drawer.

Colm: There is? What is it?

Kelly: An envelope.

Colm: Let me see that! *(He jumps up on the bar and grabs the envelope from Kelly's hands just as she's pried it from the drawer.)*

Kelly: Hey now, Colm McGinty!

Colm tears open the envelope.

One Lucky Night

Colm: *(Laughing in rapture)* This is it! This is it! It's been here this whole time!!!!

Kelly: What is it?

Colm: *(Showing Kelly a document.)* It's a horse! A thoroughbred!

Kelly: It looks like a piece of paper to me, Colm.

Colm: Kelly, it's the deed to a thoroughbred race horse. A winner!

Kelly: What??

Hugh comes over to the bar.

Colm: Yes! You always thought your da lost his life's saving that last day at the races.

Hugh: Thanks to you, Colm.

Colm: But he didn't. He won that day!

Kelly: What?!?

Colm: He had all his savings, yes, and he bet on a horse, but the horse *won!*

Hugh: You're full of it.

Colm: No. It was the strangest thing. I remember every bit of it. Old Kelly always had a feel for the horse, you know. But this day, he felt something strange. We were just about to place our bets, when Kelly stopped, and said he saw an old friend across the way. Said he had to talk to him before he placed his bet. So he went off.

Kelly: Who was this friend?

Colm: I don't know for sure. He was far away and I didn't get a good look at him. But I could tell he was not that tall, and slight of build... with dark hair....Anyway, Kelly came back, beaming. He had this big smile on his face, and a gleam in his eye that I hadn't seen since...since....

Kelly: Since the day Mother died.

Colm: He marched right up to the window and put his entire savings down on one horse. To win. I tried like the dickens to stop him; told him it wasn't prudent—

Hugh: You know the word "prudent"?

Colm: But he was so strong of mind. He placed the bet. *(Pause)* And the horse, she won.

Kelly: How—how much money was the purse?

Colm: *(Pause)* One million, seven hundred and fifty thousand dollars. And then he bough the horse, right after the race!

Kelly: How much did it cost?

Colm: A clean one million.

Kelly: *(She sits.)* A million... that means....

Hugh: I don't believe a word of it.

Colm grabs the deed and shoves it in Hugh's face. Hugh sits on a barstool, looking at the deed.

Colm: Hey, there's something else in the envelope, too.... It's a will!

Hugh & Kelly: A will??

Colm: *(Reading and crossing to front of bar. Kelly follows him.)* Murmur murmur blah blah murmur—oh, faith.....

Kelly: What is it?

Colm: He... he....

Kelly: What? *(She grabs the will.)* Oh.

Hugh: What? What??

Kelly: He gave the horse to Colm. And to me.

Lonnie: A wedding present.

Kelly and Colm look at Lonnie.

Kelly: A what?

Lonnie: He gave the horse to you and Colm as a wedding gift. He wanted the two of you to get married, and have the type of love that he shared with your beautiful mother, Agnes.

Kelly: You... you knew her, didn't you?

Lonnie: Yes. Una and I used to come here many, many years ago. We were here the night your father met your mother.

Kelly: You were?

Una: Aye. Lonnie and I always said that they were made for each other. There was a charge in the air like magic when they were in the room together.

Lonnie: I've known a number of you forebears, Moira Kelly. Beauty runs strong in your family.

Una: Oh, don't start going on about what a stud you were in your younger days.

Lonnie: You know they were all before you, my heart. Colm, what was the name of the horse that Kelly bet on?

Colm: Lucky. Short for Luck o' the Irish.

Lonnie: Blast! I told him to place the bet on High Pockets. I definitely told him *not* to bet on Luck o' the Irish!

Una: He must have known that you'd confirm which horse *not* to bet on. A fair cobbler might you be, Avalon O'Shea, but a horseman, you're certainly not.

Colm looks at Lonnie and Una, then at Kelly. He crosses to her.

Kelly: Colm, about...what I said...I...I didn't-- *(Colm gets down on one knee.)* What do ya think you're—

Colm: Moira Kelly, hush a moment. Moira Kelly, I love you. I have loved you from that Sunday night long ago, when Old Kelly brought be home to have dinner with his family. I thought he was just taking pity on a poor street kid. But he brought me to his home to be part of his family. I don't know whether he knew that I'd fall deeply, passionately in love with you the moment my eyes beheld that stern look you gave me, but I did. I will cherish you all of my days, Moira Kelly. Will you be my wife? Will you marry me, Moira?

Kelly: *(Pause)* Yes—oh, yes, Colm! *(She falls into his arms, kissing him and crying.)*

Hugh: St. Peter's Beard! I'm rich!

Colm: What?

Hugh: Dad left me the remainder of his winnings! Seven hundred and fifty thousand dollars!

Kelly: Oh, Hugh, that's marvelous!

Hugh: And the first thing I'm going to do is pay off the mortgage on this building, Moira. This'll be Kelly's Irish Rose forever.

Kelly: Oh, I don't know. Doesn't "McGinty's Ale House" have a nice ring to it?

Colm: No. Kelly's it is, and Kelly's it shall be. Your father and may have passed on, but it feels like they haven't gone too far. This must always be a home for the Kellys.

Hugh crosses to Colm.

Hugh: I...I always felt like you took my place, Colm. But now I realize that I cut myself off from Dad.

Colm: He always loved you, Hugh.

Hugh: I know that, now.

Colm: And he always wanted you to live your own life, the way you wanted to. He told me that many times.

Hugh: There's so much time lost. So much to make up...

Lonnie: There's no time like the present to start.

Enter Paul.

Paul: Hi, again!

Hugh: You're a persistent one, aren't ya?

Paul: *(Beaming)* It's one of my many great qualities. I like a gruff exterior, especially when it covers such a softy on the inside.

Una: Hey, don't you work at the Shillelagh?

Paul: Yes! Hey, you're Una! I love your music! Oh, my god!

Una: And I love the Shillelagh. They play *great* music. Not my music, but great nonetheless. A gay Irish bar! What'll they think of next?

Paul: *(To Hugh)* So...have you changed your mind about the dance contest?

Hugh: I do feel like dancing, now that I've got these wonderful new shoes. *(He puts on his shoes.)* And you know what? I'll buy *you* a drink tonight.

Paul: Wow! Handsome *and* generous!

Una: Awww... you two are so cute together!

Colm: Well, this looks like a fine time for a celebration. Round of pints, then!

Kelly: For once, Colm McGinty, you've said something worth repeating. *(They kiss.)* Pints all around, on the house!

People begin pouring in through the front door, loudly and cheerfully. Kelly begins to pour pints. Colm hands them to everyone.

Blackout.

www.ingramcontent.com/pod-product-compliance
Lightning Source LLC
LaVergne TN
LVHW041459070426
835507LV00009B/685